Camp is for the Camper

A Counselor's Guide to Youth Development

Connie C. Coutellier
Kathleen Henchey

American Camping Association®

American Camping Association, Inc.
5000 State Road 67, North
Martinsville, Indiana 46151-7902
765-342-8456 American Camping Association National Office
800-428-CAMP American Camping Association Bookstore
www.ACAcamps.org

Library of Congress Cataloging-in-Publication Data
Coutellier, Connie.
    Camp is for the camper: a counselor's guide to youth
    development/Connie L. Coutellier and Kathleen Henchey.
        p. cm.
    Includes index.
    ISBN 0-87603-168-8
    1. Camp counselors — United States. 2. Children —
    Counseling of — United States — Handbooks, manuals, etc.
    3. Youth — Counseling of — United States — Handbooks,
    manuals, etc. I. Henchey, Kathleen, 1950-II. Title.
    GV198.C6 C68 2000
    796.54'01'9 — dc21   00-021186

Cover photo courtesy of Kamp Kiwani, Middleton, Tennessee

Table of Contents

About This Booklet

This booklet is designed to help you discuss preventions and interventions with your director and other counselors and to teach you:

- responsibilities as role model
- tips to survive the stress of your first experiences supervising a camper group
- characteristics and program considerations for your camper age group
- suggestions for reinforcing positive behaviors and for dealing with inappropriate behaviors of individual campers and camper groups

The purpose of this booklet is to provide a resource to assist camp counselors in working more effectively with their campers. The authors have gathered information through discussions with camp directors, workshops, and years of their own practical experience as camping professionals. This booklet serves as a discussion starter in counselor training. The camp will need to identify specific policies and procedures, as well as the appropriate and inappropriate behaviors pertaining to their camp and clientele. The authors and the American Camping Association encourage counselors or camp personnel to seek additional information and training.

Authors

Connie Coutellier is the director of professional development for the American Camping Association, a trainer, and author of books and articles including The *Management of Risks and Emergencies* and the *Outdoor Book* both published by Camp Fire, Inc. She has over fifteen years of experience as a camp director and over twenty-five years of experience training directors and program administration staff. She designed the ACA professional development plan and worked with volunteers to develop the curriculum for ACA camp director courses.

Kathleen Henchey, is a manager in the professional development department of the American Camping Association, providing research and training to directors and staff. Kathy is the coordinator for ACA's Outdoor Living Skills program. She has six years of experience as a director and ten years in other camp staff positions.

Disclaimer

This book provides an overview of issues with which camp counselors should be familiar. It should be recognized that camp staff who lead campers may require further education and experience in each of the areas covered herein. Neither the publisher nor the author of this book undertake to verify that individuals who use this book are trained appropriately. Nor do the publisher or authors assume any responsibility for liability for any consequences of the use of information in this book. Further, the American Camping Association, Inc. and the authors hereby expressly disclaim any responsibility, liability, or duty to camp administrators, operators, personnel, any program participants or their families, for any such liability arising out of injury, illness, or loss to any person or organization.

Chapter 1

A Unique Opportunity

Camp — What a great job! What fun! What a rush! Spending your summer at camp doing outdoor activities with campers gives you a unique opportunity to contribute to the growth and development of the children in your care. You have been hired because your director believes you are capable of using good judgement, demonstrating teamwork, having concern for others, and making a positive contribution to campers and the camp community.

The Camp Environment

The camp community is unique. It is a community of persons living together as an organized, democratic group in an outdoor setting. Similar to society, a camp community takes shape in small groups like family groups that are part of a larger unit or neighborhood. These neighborhoods join to form a self-contained group known as a camp community. Staff, in a variety of roles, provide trained leadership to make the community function effectively. While camp is an informal and intense experience, it is in a relaxed, open atmosphere that provides adventure, fun, and relief from the daily pressures and stresses of the home community.

Responsibility as a Role Model

Your status is also unique. You have neither the rights of a parent nor the responsibilities of a director, yet you exert tremendous influence on campers through your close contact with them. Your influence is extremely important because children tend to imitate their adult role models. The example you set reflects your own values, expectations, background, and experiences. Parents have entrusted their most precious possession — their child — to you. They are allowing you to be their partner in the development of their child. Realizing that their child is looking up to you, they expect you to not only provide a safe and enjoyable experience, but to help their child develop the skills necessary to become caring, competent, and successful adults.

Camp Gives Kids a World of Good

Each camp has specific goals and desired outcomes for its campers. Beyond providing a fun and safe outdoor experience for children, camps contribute to the development of life skills, which are the skills children need to become responsible citizens. These competencies are best achieved when the camp provides opportunities for:

- meaningful relationships with positive role models
- exploration of self and the environment
- informal interaction with peers
- experiences that are inherently interesting and fun
- physical activity
- safe experiences with limits and supervision
- structured reflection on the experience

It is important that you understand your camp's purpose, goals, and desired outcomes for the campers in your care. Review the camp brochure and discuss what your camp has promised parents. Know what your role is in accomplishing these outcomes and how you are expected to contribute.

First Sight/Arrival

Don't panic! The most important time to establish a positive relationship with your campers and help them become comfortable is during your first meeting. As you are checking out your camper group, they are sizing you up, too. They are asking themselves, "Will this person care about me, be on my side, and are we going to play, work, and be friends?"

Here's what you can do to make campers feel at ease:

- Smile, be enthusiastic and cheerful.
- Look them in the eye and say their name.
- Make campers feel important by letting them know you are happy they are at camp.
- Help them say good-bye to their parents and join their camper group.
- Start a conversation with them; find out what makes them unique, what they like, and what they want to do at camp.
- Try to get to know each camper and help them get to know the other members of their group.

The First Day/Night

The first day's events set the tone for the rest of the campers' stay at camp. Be sure that campers know how their needs will be met. When all campers arrive, have several age-appropriate, get-acquainted games ready to play. Plan activities that have the group work as a team. Schedule a tour of camp and when campers are feeling comfortable with their surroundings and each other, it is time to discuss the schedule for the next day(s) at camp. Discuss what they will be doing and when. Talk to them about the rules that they will need to follow so that everyone will have fun and a safe time at camp.

If you are working at a resident camp, preparing for bedtime on the first night is difficult for everyone. You have probably just returned from a break and have tried to cram everything you needed to do in a twenty-four hour period. New campers have arrived and are worried, scared, or worse — missing home (homesick). This is when you will need all the patience you have and more. Plan an evening activity that starts out very active and finishes up with a quiet exercise such as reading or telling stories. Nothing scary. This is a good time to talk about what night noises they might hear and what those noises are. When you have reassured the group and answered all of their questions and concerns, it's time for bed. Spend some time with each camper to determine whether or not you have calmed fears and made him or her comfortable for the night.

Stress 24/7

To say camp is an intense experience is probably like saying you can't camp without marshmallows. Camp possesses you and the camper completely; you are at camp with almost no outside influences or distractions. A camp counselor may spend as much or more time with campers than campers' parents are able to spend. Particularly in the resident camp situation where staff members are often with campers twenty-four hours a day, day after day. Even with time off, a counselor can find him or herself burnt out by the end of the fourth or fifth week of camp. Time off may actually cause additional stress when pressured to be with friends, do laundry, drive distances, etc. Living in close quarters with others while preforming demanding and physically challenging duties can lead to a decrease in one's tolerance level. When you are exhausted or getting angry at campers and other staff, you can take the following steps to reduce stress and enjoy the summer:

- Make sure you get enough sleep.
- Maintain a good sense of humor.
- Eat well.
- Make time for yourself.
- Recognize your limits.
- Find someone in whom you can confide.
- Resolve problems quickly.
- Be patient with other staff members, campers, and yourself.

Child Abuse

Camp is a place where campers find adults they can trust and admire. Your campers may confide abusive behavior (i.e., physical, sexual, and/or psychological) that has occurred in the home environment or abusive behaviors by other staff or campers. Some signs of psychological abuse (withdrawal, lack of self-esteem or self worth, constant need for approval, etc.) or sexual abuse (inappropriate sex play, unusual knowledge of sex for the child's age, etc.) may be dismissed as other types of behavior or normal human growth and development. Other symptoms of child abuse identified by the National Center for Missing or Exploited Children include:

- "Changes in behavior, extreme mood swings, withdrawal, fearfulness, and excessive crying

- Bed-wetting, nightmares, fear of going to bed, or wearing lots of clothes to bed

- Acting out inappropriate sexual activity or showing unusual interest in sexual matters

- Regression to infantile behavior

- A sudden acting out of feelings or aggressive or rebellious behavior

- A fear of certain places, people, or activities, especially of being alone with certain people

- Pain, itching, bleeding, fluid, or rawness in the private areas"

Camp may also be a place where adults can build trusting relationships with campers. Your director will explain any policies regarding appropriate and inappropriate touch in camp, how to handle any suspicion of abuse before or during camp, and policies concerning contact with campers after camp. Some general guidelines for counselor behavior with campers are:

- Never touch a child against the child's will (verbally or nonverbally expressed) unless it is to prevent an accident.

- When others are present, it is usually okay to touch a child on the shoulders, arm, or upper back.

- Excessively tickling, wrestling with, or teasing a camper is inappropriate.

- It is inappropriate to share information about your personal sexuality or sex life.

- Don't show favoritism or encourage crushes or romantic fantasies that campers may have about you.

- Respect the privacy of campers during the times when they are changing clothes or showering.

11

- Young campers should be encouraged to change their own clothes.
- It is not appropriate to share a bed or sleeping bag with a camper.
- Don't show signs of affection to other staff in front of campers. Remember: Camp is for the camper.

Directors carefully screen staff by securing references and background checks, but if a child confides in you about another camper or staff member, discuss the disclosure personally with the director and refrain from investigating or discussing it with other staff. In most states, a camp's staff have a legal obligation to report child abuse to the authorities. The increase in camper-to-camper abuse is discussed in the section on group behavior. What may have been considered a prank or hazing in the past is often considered abuse today.

Chapter 2

Today's Campers

Bob Ditter, a child and family therapist and speaker specializing in child and adolescent treatment, states in his book, *In the Trenches*, "Today, as never before, camping is in a position to be a pivotal player in the growth and development of children. To realize this potential, camping professionals must become more aware of the social and emotional needs of both children and parents." He also speaks of the growing "emotional baggage" campers bring to camp. Campers are in the business of growing up. They are developing competencies, trying on new roles, learning social skills, and trying to control their feelings and impulses.

Social Trends

Technological advances, family dynamics, and changing populations impact camps and the children they serve. To better understand the behavior and background of your campers, you should be aware of the following social trends:

- Communication expectations of parents have changed with available technology. Campers often receive letters via fax and e-mail.

- Both the proportion of children living in extreme poverty and those living in families with high income continues to increase causing a growing income disparity among families with children and a decrease in the number of middle class families. (ChildStats)

- One in three children born in 1997 was born to a single mom and one third of those mothers are teenagers. (United States Department of Health and Human Services [USDHHS])

- About 28 percent of families are headed by a single parent. (U.S. Census) Among children living with their mothers, nearly three quarters of the mothers work.

- By 2000, 33 percent of America's total population will be African American, Latino, and Asian American. (U.S. Census)

- From ages four to five, children stereotype gender behavior, express racial reasons for not playing with others, and show discomfort around people with disabilities. Between the ages of seven and nine, children develop what psychologists call "true racial attitudes," likely to be long lasting. (National Public Radio's teacher guide, "Prejudice Puzzle")

- More children have experienced violence in their lives and are responding aggressively.

- Children spend nearly half of their discretionary time watching television. (Child Trends, Inc., USDHHS)

- The amount of time children spend on the Internet is increasing at a very rapid rate.

- The rates of asthma and chronic bronchitis in children increased over 75 percent from 1982 to 1993. (Child Trends, Inc., USDHHS)

- ADHD affects 3 to 5 percent of the children in this country. (USDHHS)

- Before they are eighteen years of age, almost half of the children born today will have parents who divorce.

So, what does this mean for the campers you will be working with? Take a few minutes to consider each statement.

Parent Interaction or Interference

The social trends listed above describe common characteristics of families in the United States today. As our society grows more complex and lifestyles become more hectic, parents are struggling with deciding what is the right thing to do for their children. Most parents want a camp experience that will provide the kind of independent, healthy growth experience their child needs, but even more importantly, they want an experience that will be safe. For most children (and their parents) the transition from home to camp involves a period of adjustment that may even include some separation anxiety. The child must learn to function in a new setting without their parents. As the time for camp arrives, the child may begin to feel anxious about leaving the comfort of a predictable environment. Parents, then, also begin to question their decision about sending their child away to camp. They want to know more about the person who will be taking care of their child.

While you may feel that the adjustment to camp would be easier if there was less contact, parents today, expect a different level of communication. Camps are trying to create a partnership with parents regarding the healthy development of their child. Be sure you understand your role in this partnership. Parents put their trust in you and have valuable information to share about their child. They don't expect you to be perfect. They do expect you to use good judgement, be attentive, and create an emotionally and physically safe environment for their child. If you have the opportunity to meet the parents or to talk with them during the session, it is important that you show real interest in their concerns and discuss ways to help their child have a successful camp experience. At the end of a camp session, don't be so anxious to begin your time off. Take a few minutes to talk to each parent and answer questions about their child's experience at camp.

Developmental Characteristics

Children are impressionable, flexible, easily led, understanding, occasionally cruel, more honest than they may ever again be, enthusiastic, at times frightened and insecure, eager for acceptance, success, adventure and fun, and have a strong need for understanding leadership. Children's behavior is not always consistent. A child can be charming and appealing for one moment, and the next moment he or she seems to be a real "pain in the neck." Although not all children fit perfectly, the following chart will give you some ideas about the physical, social, emotional, and intellectual characteristics of the age groups you will be working with. There are also some suggestions for activities and special considerations for each age group.

AGE CHARACTERISTICS CHART

FIVE TO SEVEN YEAR OLDS

Physical
- mastering physical skills (physical activities)
- better control of large muscles than small muscles
- high activity level (restless and fidgety)
- working on eye-hand coordination

Social
- learning to be friends and have "best" friends
- becoming more aware of peers and their opinions
- beginning to experience empathy for others
- still family oriented (beginning to relate to non-family adults)
- becoming aware of sexual differences
- want to structure their environment as home is structured
- want assurance of an adult's presence

Emotional
- see fairness as being nice to others so they will be nice in return
- seek parent and adult approval
- behave in ways to avoid punishment
- developing modesty
- expressing feelings and emotions, upsets are usually short-term

Intellectual
- increasing attention span (activities best limited to fifteen to thirty minutes)
- more interested in process than product
- learning to sort things into categories and arrange in a series
- learning concepts of right and wrong, cause and effect
- handle well only one mental operation at a time
- can distinguish between reality and fantasy, but may be afraid of scary figures

Activities and Special Considerations

Provide opportunities for:

- experimentation using bodies, ideas, and material in different ways
- active, boisterous games, climbing and balance, rhythmic activities
- practicing skills in eye-hand coordination such as cutting, pasting, drawing, etc.
- practice in group cooperation, sharing, and good work habits
- freedom to do things for themselves (no longer babies) and use and develop their own abilities
- use of senses requiring use of ears, eyes, nose, mouth, and skin
- reenacting routines and events of their known world
- developing friendship skills of sharing, helping, taking turns, and working with others
- finding appropriate ways of channeling emotions and behaviors

❏　❏　❏

EIGHT TO TEN YEAR OLDS

Physical

- experience steady increases in large muscle development
- increased strength, balance, and coordination
- active with boundless energy, often restless and fidgety
- boys and girls maturing at differing rates (boys are slower to mature)
- increasing in manual dexterity, eye-hand, and small muscle coordination

Social

- sees adults as authority
- follows rules out of respect for authority

- can be noisy and argumentative
- feels loyalty to friendship group, often with "secret" words
- identifies with same sex group
- expanded use of reasoning skills to solve problems, negotiate, and compromise

Emotional

- view right behavior as "obeying" rules set by those in power
- accepts parent/family beliefs
- admires and imitates older boys and girls
- developing decision making skills
- beginning to take responsibility for their own actions
- needs acceptance from peer groups
- emphasizes similarities between self and friends
- looks to adults for guidance and approval
- needs involvement with caring adult
- comparisons with the success of others difficult and eroding of self-confidence
- self-conscious, afraid to fail, sensitive to criticism
- feel they can do no wrong and are quick to correct others
- name-calling and teasing are methods for responding to being upset
- feel too "cool" for emotions

Intellectual

- quick, eager, and enthusiastic
- vary greatly in academic abilities, interests, and reasoning skills
- increased attention span, but interests change rapidly
- beginning to think logically and symbolically
- learning to use good judgement
- beginning to learn about moral judgments, applying principles of right and wrong
- wants to know how to, what, and why of things
- see things as "black and white" and "yes and no" and have difficulty with opinions different than theirs

Activities and Special Considerations

Provide opportunities for:

- using large and small muscles in activities
- organized team games and sports where everyone can be successful
- to work in groups in cooperative activities
- to use skills to explore and investigate the world
- assuming responsibility
- discuss other people's viewpoints
- to explore interests in collections and hobbies
- express feelings and imagination through creative writing or acting
- discussing reasonable explanations for rules and decisions
- interested in making and doing "real" things and using "real" tools, equipment, and materials

❏ ❏ ❏

ELEVEN TO THIRTEEN YEAR OLDS

Physical

- exhibit a wide range of sexual maturity and growth patterns between genders and within gender groups (girls are about two years ahead of boys)
- rapid change in physical appearance
- growth of hands and feet, nose and ears my be faster than arms and legs and face causing concern for appearance
- may try experimental behavior to enhance sensory stimulation, e.g., drug and alcohol use

Social

- shifting from emphasis on same sex to opposite sex — girls develop interest in boys earlier than boys in girls
- looking more toward peers than parents, seek peer recognition
- seek acceptance and trust

- tend to regard sex in a depersonalized way
- search for adult role models and often identify with admired adult hairdos, dress, and mannerisms of popular sports and music stars
- question authority
- question family values
- willing to submerge self for benefit of group
- discipline can be a problem because of spirit of group
- friendship groups or cliques are often small but intense
- more realistic understanding of who they are and what they can do
- more interested in social activities

Emotional
- compare themselves to others
- concerned about development and emerging sexually
- see themselves as always on center stage
- conscious about bodily changes
- concerned about being liked by friends, social graces, grooming
- strive for independence, yet want and need parent help
- seek privacy from parents/adults
- want to be a part of something important
- aware of degrees of emotion and seek to find the right words to describe their feelings
- exaggeration and sarcasm are frequently used to describe subtle meanings

Intellectual
- need information for making decisions
- find justice and equality to be important issues
- think abstractly and hypothetically
- can solve problems that have more than one variable
- can imagine consequences
- ready for in-depth, long-term experiences
- have moved from fantasy to realistic focus on their life's goals

Activities and Special Considerations

Provide opportunities for:

- more structured and adult-like activities
- explore other cultures, foods, languages, and customs
- completing projects (emphasis on precision and perfecting)
- discuss issues and opposite sex with friends
- opportunities to making decisions
- fun, learning experiences
- interested in activities involving the opposite sex and learning to deal with opposite sex

❏   ❏   ❏

FOURTEEN TO SEVENTEEN YEAR OLDS

Physical

- sexual maturity, with accompanying physical and emotional changes
- concerned about body image, may have complexion problems
- smaller range in size and maturity among peers
- tend to have realistic view of limits to which body can be tested
- desire to do things that give an adrenaline rush, or the extraordinary
- boys have enormous appetites; girls tend to watch weight

Social

- achieving independence from family
- tend to romanticize sexually, but moving toward more realistic understanding
- search for intimacy
- prefer to set own goals rather than accept those set by others
- more accepting of differences
- makes and keeps commitments
- see adults as fallible
- renegotiate relationships
- want adult leadership roles

Emotional

- strong identification with admired adult
- desire respect
- beginning to accept and enjoy their own individuality, but still seek status and approval of peer group
- take on multiple roles
- are introspective
- can see self from the viewpoint of others
- can initiate and carry out their own tasks without supervision of others
- desire a role in determining what happens in their world

Intellectual

- beginning of occupational choice
- want their point of view heard
- enjoy demonstrating acquired knowledge
- develop theories to explain how things happen
- will lose patience with meaningless activity
- good problem solvers but are frustrated when not consulted
- can better understand moral principles
- idealistic view of adult life
- beginning to think of leaving home for college, employment, marriage

---

Activities and Special Considerations

Provide opportunities to:

- be a part of the decision making process
- be empowered to make a difference in what's happening
- show and value their individual differences
- take on responsibility for others
- be a part of coeducational activities
- apply leadership skills
- demonstrate self-expression
- discuss issues and values

❑ ❑ ❑

ADULTS AND SENIOR CITIZENS

Young Adult Characteristics (18-26)

- becoming independent and making it on their own
- focusing on developing marketable skills and knowledge to earn a living
- rather idealistic view of adult life
- formulating values and developing a philosophy of life
- beginning to focus on choosing a mate
- interested in expanding base of experiences — travel, vocational experiences, etc.

Adult Characteristics

- achieving satisfaction in one's vocation
- assuming social and civic responsibilities
- developing skills that are family-centered
- becoming parents and raising children to become responsible and well adjusted
- learning to relate to (or care for) parents and older adults
- testing and refining values
- learning to cope with anxiety and frustration
- more financial pressures
- increased family and work-related stress
- expect housing that will provide some privacy and comfort

Senior Citizens' Characteristics

- adjusting to declining energy and physical changes of aging, i.e., decreased flexibility, balance, auditory and visual problems, less strength and endurance, slower reaction time
- building new relationships with grown children and grandchildren
- learning to relate again to one's spouse
- coming to terms with one's life goals and aspirations
- principled moral reasoning
- may have less financial pressure
- may have a more conservative outlook on life than younger adults
- expect housing that will provide privacy and accessibility

Chapter 3

Working with Individual Campers

Children want to be well-liked, to be part of the group, and to seek your approval. It is normal for you to like one camper better than another, as long as you try to treat all campers as fairly as possible. Children imitate the behavior of those who are important to them, without judging whether the behavior is positive or negative. Staff members need to be sure that their individual behavior is worth being copied.

Reinforcing Positive Behaviors

As a camp leader, you can encourage good behavior in a number of positive ways:

- Establish a caring relationship with campers by opening lines of communication and inviting a camper to come to you if they have a problem.

- Praise campers to encourage positive behavior. When counselors praise positive acts and ignore negative ones, the message is sent that campers must behave in a positive way to gain attention.

- Create an atmosphere of cooperation and fun.

Good behavior management helps the camper know his or her limits, helps you deliver a quality program, provides time for your attention to each child, helps the camp provide a safe experience, and meets the expectations of parents.

Manners

Today many children rarely have a sit-down family dinner where they learn basic table manners or the informal group interactions necessary for group living. Although campers come from a variety of backgrounds and family experiences, an agreed upon set of manners can help teach respect for others, common courtesies, and basic social skills. These manners could be expressed as rules; for example, don't litter, be on time, don't interrupt when others are talking, etc. When you discuss conduct based on how we should function as a community, the learning is more meaningful than simply a list of rules. Rules may be set by the camp or decided upon by the group. When setting rules of conduct, discuss such questions as:

- What manners are to be observed in the dining area and why are they important? Be sure to include passing and sharing food, when they can begin eating, when they are dismissed, appropriate table conversation, sitting at the table, and noise levels, along with information on how the food is served and how the tables are prepared and cleaned up.

- How do we treat each other's belongings?

- What manners should campers show each other?

- What courtesies should we show to people who have provided the food, keep the site maintained, provide program or health care, etc.?

Understanding Behavior Clues

If a camper is misbehaving, try to understand why the child's behavior is a problem. They may have a personality trait, a behavior that irritates you or other campers, or it may be a clue to a bigger problem. This problem may or may not be known by the child. Some behaviors are **overt actions** such as teasing or bullying, using obscene language, showing off, etc. Some behaviors may be **reactions** to you, other campers, or the camp environment. Reactions include fear, crying, stubbornness, timidity, acts of retaliation, etc. Lastly, some inappropriate behaviors are **practices** such as nail biting, poor speech, masturbation, bed-wetting, etc. They may happen first while at camp and/or be something for which the child is being treated. It is important that you are aware of any isotropic medications or notes from parents that may help you deal with the behavior appropriately.

Missing Home (Homesick)

Nearly 95 percent of campers have some feeling of missing home, which is a distress or impairment caused by an actual or anticipated separation from home. Missing home is characterized by acute longing and preoccupying thoughts of home. Many youngsters miss parents, friends, home, or pets and become despondent and tearful. The term missing home is replacing the older term homesick; children are not sick. One of the best preventive measures is to raise the campers' comfort levels right from the start. Make sure they feel welcome and know what will be happening on the first day.

Bed-wetting

It is not unusual for younger campers to be faced with the embarrassing situation of bed-wetting in the resident camp setting. Bed-wetting is not a behavioral problem. No child wants to wake up in a wet bed. Camp is not the place to try to remedy the problem. The role of the counselor is to avoid embarrassment or humiliation of the camper before his or her peers. A procedure for handling the clothes and bedding should be developed so that counselors can deal with this quietly and sensitively without any punishment to the camper. Counselors can also help the child by encouraging them to limit fluid intake after dinner and reminding all campers to go to the bathroom before going to bed. Counselors can also wake the child in the night and walk them to the bathroom.

Neither is it unusual for younger campers to "soil" themselves in the process of play or excitement. Again the key to the situation is to avoid embarrassment or humiliation. The counselor may also help the situation by encouraging a regular time for a bowel movement or reminding the youngster about going to the toilet.

Aggression and Violence

Incidents in schools and elsewhere of violence, weapons possession, and threats against others have brought a heightened concern for these problems in camp. It is important that staff be trained to recognize warning signs that may precede acts of violence both in themselves and in others. Although there is no foolproof system for identifying potentially dangerous youngsters, The National School Safety Center identified some behaviors that could indicate a youth's potential for harming him or herself or others:

■ engaging in tantrums, serious disciplinary problems, and uncontrollable angry outbursts

■ name calling, cursing, and abusive language

■ making violent threats

■ having few or no close friends

■ being preoccupied with weapons

■ being bullied or bullying peers or younger children

■ preferring movies and reading materials dealing with violent themes or rituals

■ participating in a gang or an antisocial group on the fringe of peer acceptance

■ demonstrating significant mood swings

■ threatening suicide

Suicide

Suicide is the third leading cause of death for persons between the ages of ten and sixteen. Counselors should be alert to signs of depression and the types of symptoms that often precede suicidal behavior. Your camp director probably has procedures for handling such behaviors and knows where to find professional help and resources. A camper or staff member that is exhibiting warning signs may:

■ have sudden changes in behavior

■ give away prized possessions

■ threaten suicide or talk about previous suicide attempts or suicide methods

■ exhibit extreme or extended boredom

■ demonstrate reckless behavior, carelessness, or self-destructive acts

- withdraw from friends and family and loses interest in activities
- act unusually sad, discouraged, and lonely, then be suddenly calm and happy
- express feelings of hopelessness, and/or worthlessness
- be preoccupied with death (perhaps evident in written expressions or artwork)
- make statements about not being missed if he or she were gone
- have family or relationship disruptions, e.g., divorce trauma or ending of a romance
- demonstrate an unusually long grief reaction from death of a friend, loved one, or even a pet
- show physical symptoms such as eating disturbances, sleeplessness, or excessive sleeping
- experience chronic headaches or stomachaches, menstrual irregularities, apathetic appearance

Any symptomatic behavior needs to be considered serious, dealt with carefully, and discussed with the camp director and/or nurse. Make it clear to the camper or staff person that talking about thoughts and feelings is okay, express concern, listen attentively, be empathetic and not judgmental, don't promise confidentiality, stress that suicide is a permanent solution to a temporary problem, and remind them that there is help and things will get better. Most importantly, don't assume you can help them by yourself.

Behaviors and Medications

However well one understands human growth and development, there are special types of problems and situations that require some advance planning by the camp director. In an informal survey of camp directors conducted by Bob Ditter, the four major behavior concerns most often mentioned were eating disorders, ADHD, increased aggressiveness, conflict among campers, and a surge in rudeness toward adults.

ADD/ADHD

Attention Deficit Hyperactive Disorder is a combination of symptoms that include inattention, destructibility, impulsiveness, and other difficulties associated with attention. Three to five percent of children in the U.S. have ADD/ADHD. Affected boys outnumber girls three to one.

Though most children can be overactive at times, a child with ADD/ADHD may act impulsive and inattentive, race ahead, take chances, often interrupt others, and seldom persist in any activity or goal. The camper with ADD/ADHD may also be socially immature and have low self-esteem and high frustration. Such behavior requires considerable supervision. The role of the counselor is to protect the camper from his or her own actions and to try to get the child to participate in normal activities. Some children will be on medication such as Ritalin for this condition; some parents take their children off the medication for the time away from home. In such cases, it is important that the health care manager and related counselor be alerted.

Eating Disorders

Anorexia Nervosa, Bulimia, and Binge (BED) are the three eating disorders that are most familiar to the general public. These conditions tend to be more a problem for girls and are closely associated with depression, low self-esteem, and stress. Adolescent girls who are concerned about weight gain often limit their food intake to a degree that can be problematic, or they may go on eating binges, followed by inducing vomiting to rid themselves of the food. These are not problems that can be solved at camp unless there is a staff person with understanding of and training in treating these maladies. Of all the behavioral difficulties a child might have, this is one that parents are extremely likely to deny, even if confronted with the facts. Because of this parent denial and the secretive aspect of these disorders, children often arrive at camp without the director being informed of the condition.

However, any counselor should be aware of what to do if he or she believes a camper is suffering with an eating disorder. The camper may react with embarrassment or become defensive or angry. Counselors should assure the camper that they will not discuss it with other campers or counselors, but because they really care about the camper and want the camper to be happy, they will report their concern to the director or camp health care manager. The camper should be able to sense acceptance from the counselor, not shock or disappointment. The counselor should encourage the camper to share feelings at any time he or she is disturbed or upset. (Directors should also be prepared to address a staff member who is suffering from an eating disorder.)

AIDS

Although AIDS is not a behavior, the awareness to persons having the condition can lead to behavior patterns or discrimination. Persons with AIDS should be treated as normally as possible. Counselors should be prepared to deal with situations that might cause bleeding or where bleeding might occur, i.e., they should have rubber gloves available in the living quarters (or in first-aid kits when out of camp) and be trained in universal precautions. Persons with AIDS ordinarily will understand the dangers to others. If the issue arises in the living group, counselors should be prepared to educate the group to the ways in which AIDS can and cannot be spread to alleviate the fears that some campers may have.

Dealing with Inappropriate Behaviors

Most incidents and accidents come when children have free time or are "horsing around." A well-planned program, timed so children are not idle or bored while waiting on others, is key to the prevention of inappropriate behavior. Have songs or no equipment games ready to play while waiting. Be prepared for the wanderer, the camper that always finishes first (or last), changes in the weather, and unexpected delays.

Discipline is sometimes regarded as an old-fashioned word; it is also a principle that helps channel selfish interests to the welfare of the whole group. Before discipline becomes an issue, take into consideration these issues that need to be understood and accepted by anyone dealing with children:

- A child has the occasional need to test the limits.
- A child cannot always manage self-control.
- A child has a strong tendency to support the values of his/her peer group.
- A child has the right to make mistakes.
- A child has a right to be respected as an individual, regardless of unattractive attributes.

Discipline problems can be prevented by helping campers understand behavior expectations while at camp, earning campers' respect by giving respect, maintaining control, listening, reading signals, and trying to be one step ahead of them.

When discipline is required, there are a few common guidelines to keep in mind. Discipline should always be used sparingly to be effective — if you discipline constantly it becomes the accepted norm. Discipline should never be used vindictively or emotionally — never let a disciplinary problem put you off balance. Punishment, if any, should follow the deed as quickly as possible. Using work as a punishment usually creates a poor attitude toward work; the exception might be when the punishable deed created work for others. Physical punishment is not acceptable, nor is verbal abuse, which can be as destructive as physical force. (It should be noted that physical punishment or verbal abuse of a camper by a counselor or another staff member may be symptoms of stress on the part of the individual and grounds for dismissal.)

If initial attempts to control or change an unacceptable behavior have failed, these disciplinary approaches may help:

- Maintain the initiative and try to persuade the camper that it is better to conform.
- Avoid specific threats by using a broad warning of a possible course of action. Rather than saying, "If you do that again, you will be sent home," try "There are consequences for breaking camp rules or for not cooperating." A child may imagine far more fearsome punishments than you can suggest. A specific threat commits you to carry it out or back down and may even

dare the child to try you out, whereas a general warning reinforces the idea that compliance will be better than defiance.

- Involve other campers in the process. An indication that peers may not like the behavior brings in a different aspect. For example, in a situation where a group of boys were bullying a younger group, the camp director got the two groups together and, by asking questions, forced the older boys to face up to their actions. There were no threats or punishment, but the behavior changed.

- Check age characteristics to assess the level of comprehension or the motivation for obeying authority.

- Review any punishment before setting it. Does it fit the offense? For example, if one camper has peppered another's dessert, is it fair that the culprit goes without his dessert? Is punishment necessary to deter a repetition of the behavior? Any persistently antisocial behavior should not be allowed to pass without some appropriate action. Some children respond better to negative consequences while others respond better to rewards or positive reinforcement.

Look for causes of poor behavior. Avoiding difficult situations is much better than having to deal with them once they arise. Campers with too much energy can get into trouble; overtired campers are prone to react badly to provocation. If there is a camper more prone to negative behavior, try to start each day in a manner that will encourage proper behavior. Try to identify campers who might cause problems and have strategies in mind to deal with them. Creating a discipline plan will keep problems from becoming overwhelming.

The Camper Behavior Management Guide on page 34 shows intervention and prevention techniques as well as consequences and policies for specific camper behaviors.

CAMPER BEHAVIOR MANAGEMENT GUIDE

Behavior	Prevention
Aggression or violence (physical abuse — hitting, shoving, weapons)	Discuss with camper expected and unexpected behavior. Be observant, listen, and try to anticipate problems. Let campers know it's alright to tell the counselor rather than retaliate. Know expectations for intervening if there is a weapon.
Argumentative or verbally abusive	Discuss rules and expectations for handling conflicts. Discuss the inappropriate behavior such as shouting, cussing, or name calling. Reinforce appropriate behavior such as compromise, cooperation, respect for others, etc.
Boredom/lazy	Discuss with group the schedule for the day or week. Post the schedule where everyone can see what's next. Utilize camper planning or urge camper input on activities they want to do. Be sure the group gets enough sleep at night and rest during the day for their age. Be excited about the program yourself. Design the program with progression.
Bullying	Discuss expectations for behavior and how to gain cooperation from other campers. Give campers examples of appropriate ways to influence fellow campers. Even though bullies are very skilled at selecting the best time to exercise their peer terror tactics, listen and observe your group to be aware of bullying behaviors that might be happening while you are not there. Male bullies are more likely to employ physical aggression while girls are more likely to use verbal abuse. If the bully has followers, purposely plan activities to mix the group. Do not "label" a child as a bully as they may enact the role.

Intervention	Consequences & Policy
Move close to the aggressor and immediately intervene. Ask the camper(s) being threatened to move away from the situation. Discuss reasons for this behavior with each. Help campers deal with whatever prompted this behavior.	☐ Is there a camp policy? ☐ Discuss solutions with camper. ☐ Discuss with supervisor/ director. ☐ Call parents. ☐ Send home. ☐ Other
Make your requests clear and do not argue or become defensive with the camper. Stop the behavior before it turns into physical abuse. Avoid looking shocked or laughing. Ask each camper to explain the problem. Help campers see alternative ways to solve problems.	☐ Is there a camp policy? ☐ Discuss solutions with camper. ☐ Discuss with supervisor/ director. ☐ Call parents. ☐ Send home. ☐ Other
Have several games, songs, and ideas of things to do when there are slow times. Try to find a new activity or new twist in doing an activity to challenge them. Recognize their experience and give them some leadership responsibilities. Be sure they understand and perform their responsibilities in the group.	☐ Is there a camp policy? ☐ Discuss solutions with camper. ☐ Discuss with supervisor/ director. ☐ Call parents. ☐ Send home. ☐ Other
If you are able to observe the bullying behavior, immediately separate the bully from the group and any followers. Explain why the behavior is inappropriate. Stay neutral and calm. Talk to the victim about his or her feelings and any damage to person or belongings. Since most bullies lack self-esteem, give them opportunities to work with others in a positive way.	☐ Is there a camp policy? ☐ Discuss solutions with camper. ☐ Discuss with supervisor/ director. ☐ Call parents. ☐ Send home. ☐ Other.

CAMPER BEHAVIOR MANAGEMENT GUIDE

Behavior	Prevention
Constant complaining or whining	Give suggestions on appropriate ways to express your opinion. Utilize camper planning or urge camper input on activities they want to do. Don't let the whining or complaining cause you to lose patience with the child. Encourage the camper to try new things and use positive phrases instead of complaining.
Destructive to property, vandalism	Discuss with campers about respecting the property of the camp and the personal property of others. Know the camp's policy on how to handle and document destructive behaviors. Be sure campers know the consequences of destructive behavior. Explain that any valuable property should not have been brought to camp and where it can be kept until the child goes home.
Doesn't follow directions or pay attention	Make directions age-appropriate, clear, and direct. Give directions in small workable steps. With some tasks you will need to give more individual attention. Ask them to repeat the directions back to you and make sure they understand them. Reinforce attentive behavior.
Fears (rejection, being out of control, being humiliated, failing, etc.)	Campers should be assured on opening day that they are safe. Do not tell scary stories, especially to young children. Empathize with the fear as natural for someone trying something new or being in a new situation. Don't tease or ridicule the child for having the fear. Determine if there is a cause or reason for the fear and discuss the problem with the child.

Intervention	Consequences & Policy
Point out the behavior and explain how it affects others. Try to find out the reasons for complaints and address each with the child. Don't become defensive. Explain to the child that you will not respond to them when they are whining, complaining, or saying I can't do something without trying.	☐ Is there a camp policy? ☐ Discuss solutions with camper. ☐ Discuss with supervisor/ director. ☐ Call parents. ☐ Send home. ☐ Other
Find out the reason for the destruction (getting even, revenge, seeking attention, fun, power, peer pressure, etc.) and deal with the real problem. Ask campers that destroyed or defaced property to restore it or pay for it. The group behavior chart in chapter 4 may be helpful if the destruction was by a group of campers.	☐ Is there a camp policy? ☐ Discuss solutions with camper. ☐ Discuss with supervisor/ director. ☐ Call parents. ☐ Send home. ☐ Other
Be patient, flexible, and willing to work with campers on a personal basis. When teaching activities, complete one task at a time and ask the camper(s) to demonstrate their understanding. Pair a camper with another camper that can keep focused. Keep eye contact with the child when you are giving instructions.	☐ Is there a camp policy? ☐ Discuss solutions with camper. ☐ Discuss with supervisor/ director. ☐ Call parents. ☐ Send home. ☐ Other
Make sure other campers do not make fun of the camper's fear. Encourage campers to participate, but do not force the camper to participate in an activity that is uncomfortable. When a camper is afraid to try a new activity or task, break it down into small progressive steps or have him gain confidence by watching others. Pair the frightened camper with a camper that can encourage and support him or her through the experience. Give opportunities for success in activities that the camper enjoys.	☐ Is there a camp policy? ☐ Discuss solutions with camper. ☐ Discuss with supervisor/ director. ☐ Call parents. ☐ Send home. ☐ Other

CAMPER BEHAVIOR MANAGEMENT GUIDE

Behavior	Prevention
Group instigator	If the camper has followers, purposely plan activities to mix the group.
	Discuss expectations for behavior and help channel leadership into positive actions.
	Give campers examples of appropriate ways to influence fellow campers.
	Help the camper understand the consequences of his or her actions.
	Consider the reasons for the camper exercising power and influence on others.
Inappropriate language (swearing, use of sexual language)	Explain rules about inappropriate language in camp the first day.
	Don't shame or put the child down for using language that may be acceptable in their home.
	Always act as a role model by using appropriate language around children.
	Give campers examples of accepted language when expressing their disagreements.
	Complement campers when you hear them using appropriate language.
	Give them acceptable ways to voice disagreements.
Impatience	Explain teamwork and ask for ideas of what he or she could to help others who are slower or less skilled.
	If child is impatient at their own skill in doing something, have other options or give them some personal attention with small steps that will lead to success.
	Have several games, songs, and ideas of things to do when there are slow times or when they have finished before others.

Intervention	Consequences & Policy
Separate the camper from the group and discuss the inappropriate behavior and the negative results of the group's action and their leadership. Help the camper determine alternative positive ways to influence the group. Provide recognition to him or her for positive leadership.	☐ Is there a camp policy? ☐ Discuss solutions with camper. ☐ Discuss with supervisor/ director. ☐ Call parents. ☐ Send home. ☐ Other
Don't ignore or overreact by showing shock or laughing when a child uses inappropriate language. Speak calmly but firmly about the language that is appropriate at camp. Make sure you let the camper know the behavior is unacceptable in camp so that others don't think it's cool and repeat their actions. Try to find out why the camper is using inappropriate language (anger or out of not knowing better).	☐ Is there a camp policy? ☐ Discuss solutions with camper. ☐ Discuss with supervisor/ director. ☐ Call parents. ☐ Send home. ☐ Other
Discuss the camper's feelings and help him or her decide what to do when they are feeling impatient (waiting on their turn, waiting for an activity to start, or on others in their group.) Recognize and emphasize with feelings of frustration and help them deal appropriately with any anger that might come from those feelings. Discuss reasons for needing self-control, being a part of the group, why there are schedules or rules, etc. Encourage the child to complete projects successfully or to help others finish.	☐ Is there a camp policy? ☐ Discuss solutions with camper. ☐ Discuss with supervisor/ director. ☐ Call parents. ☐ Send home.

CAMPER BEHAVIOR MANAGEMENT GUIDE

Behavior	Prevention
Lying	☐ Emphasize trust and the team or group working together. ☐ Don't laugh and inadvertently reward the behavior. ☐ Model telling the truth. When you make a mistake, admit it. ☐ To promote truthfulness, consistently recognize and praise campers for honesty.
Pranks or hazing	☐ Discuss inappropriateness of pranks or hazing type activities on individuals in your camp. Most end up hurting someone either emotionally or physically and could cause a camper to be sent home or be grounds for staff dismissal. ☐ Jokes or pranks often grow out of control if left unchecked, if a joke is played on you accept it and let it die without retaliation. ☐ Be sure campers are aware of the consequences of a joke that is hurtful or destructive. ☐ Listen and give guidance to conversations that include plans for pranks or retaliation. ☐ As a role model do not instigate pranks or hazing type activities on other staff or campers.
Put others down (name calling, unkind remarks)	☐ Discuss why it is unacceptable to put others down or call them hurtful names at camp and the consequences of such behavior. ☐ Explain that racial or ethnic diversity in the group as well as different opinions contribute to the group development and should not be a target for unkind remarks. ☐ Talk about how hurtful it may feel if it happened to them. ☐ Be a good example when interacting with campers, show them respect. ☐ Move around the group and listen to how campers communicate with each other.

Intervention	Consequences & Policy
Determine the reason(s) for the behavior (attention, belonging, getting respect, etc.) and suggest more appropriate ways to deal with those feelings. Do not "set up a camper to lie" if you know they have done something wrong. Tell them you know what happened and ask for ways to remedy the situation. Talk with camper about unacceptable behavior and discuss what happens when one lies and what happens when they tell the truth. Ignore obvious exaggerations and help the camper tell the difference between reality and wishful thinking.	☐ Is there a camp policy? ☐ Discuss solutions with camper. ☐ Discuss with supervisor/ director. ☐ Call parents. ☐ Send home. ☐ Other
Help children to not react in the anticipated manner to a joke played on them. If they ignore or accept it without acknowledgment the real joke may be on the perpetrators. Jokes or pranks on counselors or on a group that are done carefully and for the campers benefit could build spirit and model how to be good sports. All adults and staff in camp behave consistently in handling incidents of pranks, jokes, or hazing type activities.	☐ Is there a camp policy? ☐ Discuss solutions with camper. ☐ Discuss with supervisor/ director. ☐ Call parents. ☐ Send home. ☐ Other
Stop the put down or name calling immediately but don't overreact. Help children to express their feelings about the action that someone does that they do not like rather than calling them a name. Do not react by laughing or ignoring the behavior thus giving camper the sense you are condoning such behavior. Correct camper in a calm voice and manner. Camper may not realize that what he or she said is not appropriate or hurtful.	☐ Is there a camp policy? ☐ Discuss solutions with camper. ☐ Discuss with supervisor/ director. ☐ Call parents. ☐ Send home. ☐ Other

CAMPER BEHAVIOR MANAGEMENT GUIDE

Behavior	Prevention
Runaway/wanderer	Discuss expectations for where they can and cannot go without a counselor and why. Try to identify why the camper leaves the group. Establish procedures for searching for a missing camper.
Stealing or borrowing without permission	Have campers mark their belongings and be responsible for keeping track of their things. Make expectations clear on the first day about use of others' belongings and care of their own belongings. Be aware of what each camper is bringing to camp, and if there is something of value either ask the parents take it home or ask the director for a safe place to keep it. Know the camp policy regarding searching a camper or staff member's belongs.
Substance abuse (smoking, alcohol, drugs)	Policies should be in the material sent to camper and parents before camp starts. Be a positive role model and follow the camp policies yourself. Do not discuss with campers whether you smoke, drink, or have ever tried drugs. Make campers aware of the camp's policies, the laws in their state, and the consequences of a camper caught with drugs, alcohol, or tobacco. Know the camp policy regarding searching a camper or staff member's belongs.

Intervention	Consequences & Policy
If the child is missing, stay calm, and keep the rest of the group calm and together. Check obvious places, ask others about when last seen, frame of mind, clothing, etc., and report as per procedures for a search. If the child is constantly wandering away from the group remind them of the rules, safety reasons for staying with the group, and consequences for continuing the behavior. Discuss the problem with whole group and ask for their help in keeping everyone together (establishing a buddy system, number off participants, and periodically ask for a call-off, etc.)	☐ Is there a camp policy? ☐ Discuss solutions with camper. ☐ Discuss with supervisor/ director. ☐ Call parents. ☐ Send home. ☐ Other
If there has been an accusation, be sensitive to both parties feelings, and try to determine if the action was stealing, a mistake, or used with or without permission. If you know who is stealing, the stolen item should be returned with an apology and the incident discussed with the director. If unsure who is stealing, have a group meeting and determine how the missing item should be returned.	☐ Is there a camp policy? ☐ Discuss solutions with camper. ☐ Discuss with supervisor/ director. ☐ Call parents. ☐ Send home. ☐ Other
Explain they have broken a camp policy and follow procedures about consequences. Be sure that you do not make premature conclusions and follow procedures about searching belongings and confiscating the materials.	☐ Is there a camp policy? ☐ Discuss solutions with camper. ☐ Discuss with supervisor/ director. ☐ Call parents. ☐ Send home. ☐ Other

CAMPER BEHAVIOR MANAGEMENT GUIDE

Behavior	Prevention
Showing-off or clowning	Do not laugh or encourage show-off behavior, explain that there may be a more appropriate time to tell the story or act in that manner. Help the campers understand expectations for accomplishing a task or activity and the time period available. Explain the importance of being serious, listening, and paying attention to instructions so that they can participate in activities or for safety reasons.
Tattling, gossip, blaming others	Discuss why it is unacceptable to gossip about others and the consequences of such behavior. Talk about how hurtful it may feel if it happened to them. Do team-building activities. Try to determine the reason for tattling on others (to win favor or to get others in trouble). Don't label the child as tattletale or gossip. Be a good example when interacting with campers, show them respect. Move around the group and listen to how campers communicate with each other.
Testing rules, limits	Make sure your rules and expectations are reasonable and coincide with camp expectations. Have the group identify their own rules for functioning safely as a group at camp. Review these rules on the first day, explain why the rule is important. Remember to be consistent in enforcing the rules and in praising campers that follow the rules.

Intervention	Consequences & Policy
Take camper aside and explain why his or her behavior is interruptive and not appropriate. Try to access the reasons for the behavior and ask for a serious answer. Try to channel the action into a positive role in a skit or other appropriate activity. Once the camper's behavior is given attention (positive or negative) by other members of the group, the behavior may be difficult for the child to control, and it may be encouraged by the other campers. A discussion with the entire group about the interruptive behavior may be necessary for the group to continue in a positive manner.	☐ Is there a camp policy? ☐ Discuss solutions with camper. ☐ Discuss with supervisor/ director. ☐ Call parents. ☐ Send home. ☐ Other
Help the camper to express their feelings appropriately about the action that someone does that they do not like. Listen to both sides of a situation and discuss more appropriate ways to handle the situation. Explain that you know they may be trying to help you but correcting others' behavior is your job. Do not ignore the behavior thus giving camper the sense you are condoning such behavior. Reward other ways to gain attention without hurting others. The camper may not realize that what he or she said is not appropriate or hurtful, or they may be struggling with the rules themselves and want their good behavior to be noticed.	☐ Is there a camp policy? ☐ Discuss solutions with camper. ☐ Discuss with supervisor/ director. ☐ Call parents. ☐ Send home. ☐ Other
Talk to the camper away from the group about his or her behavior. Review the rules with the whole group and ask for their help in reinforcing positive behavior. Give campers the opportunity to challenge rules appropriately. Meet with other staff and the director to discuss productive ways to challenge authority and how to prevent difficulties.	☐ Is there a camp policy? ☐ Discuss solutions with camper. ☐ Discuss with supervisor/ director. ☐ Call parents. ☐ Send home. ☐ Other

CAMPER BEHAVIOR MANAGEMENT GUIDE

Behavior	Prevention
Unusual sexual behavior (inappropriate touching of others or themselves, exposure, etc.)	Discuss privacy issues, personal space, and unwanted touching of other campers. Unusual sexual behavior may be an indication of sexual abuse in the home or other settings or an indication the child has been stimulated by magazines, TV, or observation of an older sister or brother. Discuss such behaviors with the director.
Victim/revenge	Discuss what to do if you are being bullied. Victims are often physically weak or emotionally vulnerable and will not seek help. Recognize that this is a difficult cycle to stop and that children can be very cruel to each other. Do teambuilding and bonding activities that put a rejected child on equal footing with others. Try to match children in the group so that they are at the same maturity level. There may be a struggle between the victim (helpless needs protection) and the popular leader for the attention of the counselor.

Intervention	Consequences & Policy
If you observe inappropriate touching of a camper by another camper, speak directly to the camper about the action. Do not assume campers know the difference between appropriate and inappropriate touch. Follow the camp's procedures for reporting and documentation of such incidents.	☐ Is there a camp policy? ☐ Discuss solutions with camper. ☐ Discuss with supervisor/director. ☐ Call parents. ☐ Send home. ☐ Other
Deal with the aggressors but realize that reprimanding the whole group may make it worse for the scapegoat. Teach the child that is being teased new ways to respond. Being angry or crying will just encourage additional attacks. Acknowledge how difficult it is to ignore teasing, make suggestions, and practice answers with him or her. The group may suggest that the scapegoat be in another group or stay with the counselor which if allowed may just perpetuate their rejection of the child. Listen and be aware of children being victimized and of any retaliation or revenge planned by the victim(s).	☐ Is there a camp policy? ☐ Discuss solutions with camper. ☐ Discuss with supervisor/director. ☐ Call parents. ☐ Send home. ☐ Other

Chapter 4

Positive Group Interaction

The uniqueness of the camp experience is more than a series of activities to engage children. It is a group-living experience. Individuals are not only brought together to share common experiences in an outdoor setting, but they are encouraged to develop a cohesive group with positive interpersonal relationships and social skills. They must develop mutual respect and trust that is greater than roles based upon one's sex, race, economic situation, or physical condition.

To successfully work with camper groups, it is important that staff agree on the appropriate and inappropriate behavior of campers, the consistent behavior management and supervisory techniques that will be employed, and the policies or consequences of inappropriate behaviors in camp. Insurance records and analysis of accidents and behavior incidents in camp are very closely tied to supervision issues, issues of what "on duty" means, free or unscheduled time, etc. The camp that enumerates a lengthy list of rules immediately upon arrival at camp invites campers to "test the limits" or violate rules. Yet, some rules are necessary in any community. The staff's method of applying those rules consistently and educating youth about the reason for the rules and gaining their participation in setting and agreeing to them is critical.

What about being a friend? From a risk-management viewpoint, as well as a control and organizational viewpoint, counselors must maintain their positions as leaders. Too often, leaders aspire to be the group's best friend and lose sight of their official role, which causes them to face decisions that compromise their responsibility and authority. Being an effective leader is a delicate weave of traits and skills: integrity, self-confidence, empathy, and the ability to foster positive group development and individual growth. The elimination of any single trait or characteristic weakens the fabric and the overall effectiveness of the leader.

The first part of this booklet identified strategies for prevention and intervention in supervising and dealing with an individual's behavior. This section will provide strategies for dealing with several group behaviors.

Setting the Tone for Group Development

In any group activity, a purpose, goal, or specific task should be identified and completed. Individuals with different talents and strengths become a group as they learn about and from each other and accept a common goal. This acceptance and common pursuit of a goal, if orchestrated properly, will supersede individual differences.

As you begin working with any group:

- Be sure the group is comfortable with each other. Start with get-acquainted activities and then progress to more personal sharing.
- Get and hold the group's attention.
- Stand or sit where everyone can see you.
- Speak just loud enough for everyone to hear you.
- Ask the group for ideas about how they should treat each other (i.e., no put-downs), listen to each other, help each other, etc.
- Participate with the group in the activities when possible.
- Listen and encourage each camper to participate and share.
- Try to make everything, even mistakes, into a learning experience.

Cycles of Group Activity Planning

Throughout the day, the session, and program activities, there are cycles that should be considered in planning:

- **Daily cycle** — Each day should be planned so that the activities are in cycles that match campers' energy level and end with settling down campers for the evening. For example, begin the day with a high-energy activity such as swimming, games, ropes course, etc. Then move campers into a more quiet and restful period with crafts, stories, thought-provoking activities or discussions, etc. After this calming period, add more high-energy activity, and end the day with quiet activities.

■ **Session cycle** — Despite the length of a camp session, it should always begin with activities that raise the comfort level within the camper group and end with returning home. (See Stages of Group Development.)

■ **Program activity cycle** — Be sure to include an introduction to each activity where the activity is explained, safety rules are discussed, and equipment gathered. Once the activity is completed, allow time to clean up and to debrief the campers on the skills or concepts learned during the program. (See Debriefing an Activity on page 55.)

Group Building

Productive group behavior is dependent on both the group's attitude and the counselor's attitude and actions. Any group should include the following attributes: guidance, organization, coordination, delegation of authority, dependability, fairness, consideration, respect, and consistency. When these qualities are present in a counselor, the morale and efficiency of the group will be higher.

As a counselor, you play a critical role in every stage of group development. The chart on page 52 depicts each stage of group development, possible group reactions, and your specific role.

STAGES OF GROUP DEVELOPMENT

Stage	Group Indicators	Counselor's Role
1. Saying hello	Feeling insecure and unsure of themselves. Being concerned about how they fit into group. Showing excitement about camp but have separation anxieties.	Clarify expectations. Build comfort with camp. Avoid discussing personal feelings or close physical contact. Encourage interaction, trust, and involvement. Use name games and icebreakers to keep group active.
2. Saying who	Sorting it out. Picking friends. Developing roles in the group. Developing norms and common ground. Getting to know how the counselor works.	Watch for power struggles and cliques. Encourage openness and sharing. Help with conflict resolution. Organize different subgroup structures for activities. Use cooperation games.
3. Saying why	Understanding their role. Building the team. Depending on each other. Beginning to work and share space together. Challenging leadership.	Help group assume responsibility for actions and decisions. Help with group decisions and problem solving. Use team-building games and group projects.
4. Saying we	Acknowledging individual strengths in each other. Developing respect for each other. Becoming interdependent. Finding success in their contribution. Sharing feelings.	Allow time for creativity and discussion. Encourage group challenge and adventure. Watch for exhaustion. Acknowledge individual and group accomplishments.
5. Saying good-bye	Having mixed feelings about leaving and going home. Recognizing growth and change. Wanting to maintain ties with camp and others in the group.	Encourage reflection. Reward accomplishments. Help transfer what they learned to home and school environment. Help with re-entry

Camper Planning

Camper or group planning as a teaching method helps the group establish a working relationship and provides a systematic approach, providing order, clarity, and purpose to their task. For example, campers that help set their own rules are more likely to follow them and help hold their group accountable for the agreed upon rules for their group.

Learning as a Part of the Group Process

Learning is more interesting and fun for campers if a variety of methods are used. The method chosen should be appropriate for the participants' ages. Some methods fit better with the subject matter being taught. For example, discussion would not be as effective as a demonstration for tying knots. Some skills can best be learned with two or more methods, for example, brainstorming ideas for safety rules, then discussing the ideas and deciding which are appropriate for the group.

Discussion, demonstration, and practice (by the counselor or a group member), observation, and idea sharing are all effective methods to use with a group. Any one method will not work for all situations or for all learners.

Discussion — Spontaneous discussion and involvement will not occur naturally if group members feel inhibited. Participation in the group discussion requires involvement, motivation to contribute, and acceptance of responsibility for one's actions.

To encourage participation in discussions:

- Praise and thank those contributing.
- Mediate differences of opinion.
- Provide the information they need for the discussion.
- Have several ideas to help them get started or to regenerate enthusiasm.
- Refocus the group's attention when necessary.
- Summarize the discussion.

Demonstration and Practice — Children learn by doing. To keep the campers' interest when you are teaching a skill, you need to be able to demonstrate the skill and have them practice it. It is hard to patiently and slowly demonstrate each step of a skill you know well and do easily. Try your demonstration first with another counselor. Be sure to:

■ Break down the demonstration into easy steps.

■ Have the group practice each step and encourage their successful progress.

■ Make the presentation fun and nonthreatening.

■ Include enough materials for each participant to be involved.

■ Repeat and review.

Observation — Many observation games or activities exist that can be used to increase campers' interest or curiosity. These teaching methods sharpen campers' skills, create excitement, and make learning fun. Use the following ideas to help your campers learn to be more observant:

■ Build on campers' observations and encourage comments.

■ Encourage campers to use all their senses.

■ Model observation by relating stories to things observed.

■ Don't rush everywhere; take time to look around you.

■ Observe from a different point of view, i.e., taking a frog's-eye view, walking backwards, or asking questions that will stimulate interest.

■ Don't worry if you don't have the answers; you can find them out together with your campers.

Generating and Sharing Ideas — In the early stages of group development, members may be shy or reluctant to share their opinions about program, rules, ways to solve a problem, planning activities, etc. To motivate campers to participate and get involved in the camper group use these steps:

■ Define the purpose of gathering ideas and the time limits.

- Set up a safe environment for generating ideas.
- Tell campers there are no bad ideas.
- Appoint someone to write ideas down.
- Discuss and prioritize the best ideas.
- If campers are older, instruct campers to pair off or gather in small groups to develop suggestions that can be reported to the whole group.

Debriefing an Activity — After completing an activity, ask group members what happened or what they learned. The leader should facilitate this discussion by encouraging and giving group members opportunities to participate. The game or activity may increase interest or curiosity and lead to other activities or discussions about how the group members worked together.

Helpful hints for debriefing:

- Build on and encourage comments.
- Use all of the senses. What did campers see, hear, feel, etc.?
- Take time to listen to campers and remind them to listen to each other.
- Ask key questions that will stimulate interest.
- It's okay not to have all the answers — learn together.
- Ask how campers will use what they learned at home.

Inappropriate Group Behavior

When dealing with a large number of youth from a variety of backgrounds and family patterns, in a setting where they can try new and different behaviors, there will be instances when those behaviors will be unacceptable and require discipline. "In every . . . camp, one of the major demands placed on directors and counselors is discipline. The key to handling this issue well is being prepared, which starts with having a plan and understanding different techniques that work."[1] The following are some of the key issues in-

---

[1]Donnie Jackson. "Disciplining Campers." *Camping Magazine* Vol. 70, No. 4, July/August 1997.

volved in group behavior and a list of suggestions for dealing with inappropriate group behavior.

Peer Pressure

Campers often need help distinguishing between needing to be part of the group and negative peer pressure. As children get older, the opinions and acceptance of their peers become more and more important. Children may ask themselves if an activity will get them into trouble, harm themselves or someone else, or if they are wanting to participate just because they don't want to be left out. The counselor can praise those campers who are willing to voice their opinions and help campers deal with peer pressure by discussing situations where it is difficult to stand against the group and why it is important to tell others how you feel.

Stereotypes/Prejudices

Children are influenced by the role models observed on television, their parents, teachers, and expectations they are comfortable with from their own culture. Camps serve different camper populations. Some are all the same sex, some target a specific economic level, religious group, or racial or ethnic group. These can be barriers to group development. People tend to act out behaviors that reinforce stereotypes or reflect their own experiences. The example you set reflects your own values, expectations, background, and experiences. It is of great importance because children tend to imitate their adult role models. Your challenge, as a counselor, is to examine your own prejudices, feelings, and actions and determine the expectations the camp has for you as a role model for their campers.

Whether you are working with a group of girls, a group of boys, or a coed group, you should be aware of several key characteristics within your camper group. In resolving conflicts, girls tend to be more verbal and boys more physical. Girls are more worried about how others feel and take criticism personally. Boys are more likely to deny feelings of vulnerability and label each other as strong or weak. Counselors need to distinguish between the stereotypical feelings of girls or boys and real conflict.

Group Rowdiness

The group can get carried away especially in the second and third stage of group development when the group is struggling for roles and testing authority. Some competitive activities over stimulate the group and lead to inappropriate group behaviors against another group. Also, negative leadership may emerge from the group during times when the group is bored or waiting, being transported, or otherwise not in structured activities. The counselor should be sensitive to what is happening in the group, and identify warning signs and ways to gain control.

Practical Jokes

Pranks and hazing are discussed in the Camper Behavior chart in chapter 3. Practical jokes can often become inappropriate group behavior as the stages of the group progresses. The joke can become something against another group, or an individual or become destructive behavior. The counselor needs to be aware of the ramifications and appropriateness of the group's behavior. Many pranks begin as team- or group-building fun and develop into retaliation and destructive behavior.

Camper-to-Camper Abuse

Camper-to-camper abuse has been a growing concern at camp and what in the past may have been considered a prank or hazing is today considered abuse. Some of the sexual behavior identified as a normal aspect of human growth and development may become abuse when a camper exhibits that behavior with a younger camper or by force on a peer. Occasionally there are children that are unable to judge the appropriateness of sexual or physical abusive behavior because of their family or personal experiences. If you have any questions about a camper's behavior, it is wise to discuss it with your camp director.

Ideas for Dealing with Inappropriate Group Behaviors

■ Explain the reason for camp rules, and ask the group to establish some group rules.

■ Listen to what the campers are saying not just how they are acting.

■ Don't be judgmental and look for the cause of the behavior.

■ Support campers as they try to find a solution.

■ Model the behavior you want to see in your campers.

■ Deliberately mix campers into different subgroups.

■ Talk with campers in a nonshaming, nonaccusatory way.

■ Explain that it is normal to have different opinions and the importance of respecting the opinion of others.

■ Help campers discuss feelings of anger, resentment, not belonging, power, fear, shame, etc.

■ Discuss what it means to be a friend and what it means to be a part of the group.

■ Play cooperative and team-building games.

■ Talk to other counselors and administrative staff about the problems you are having with your group.

Chapter 5

How to Measure Your Success

This booklet along with your training and experience have helped prepare you to be able to reinforce positive or appropriate behaviors and deal with the inappropriate ones. Don't wait until the end of camp to look at how successful you are with your campers. And, occasionally take a look at your attitude and actions that might contribute to your success.

Does your attitude need adjusting? Now that you have some experience in working with campers and other staff, the following points may help you examine your feelings and become more effective:

- Attitude is contagious — Be optimistic and make it your goal to help campers begin each day with a positive attitude.

- Share your expectations — Help campers understand expectations for behavior while at camp and reinforce positive behaviors.

- Problems have a way of growing — Set goals to prevent problems and then promptly deal with inappropriate behaviors.

- Earn the respect of your campers by giving respect — Treat the behavior of campers consistently, be fair, maintain control, listen and read signals and try to be one step ahead of them.

- Share your struggles — Look for ways to work with other staff on a solution to behavior problems you may be having with your campers and share your successes.

Evaluating Your Success as a Counselor

Periodically do a self-assessment to rate how you are handling stress and dealing with your campers. Use the following scale to rate how you were feeling: 1 = always, 2 = most of the time, 3 = sometimes, 4 = rarely.

___ Did I have an overall feeling of success at meeting the camp's goals and outcomes for campers?

___ Did I personally interact and participate with campers?

___ Did I handle behavior problems promptly, fairly, and consistently?

___ Can I control my temper and keep from getting impatient with campers and other staff?

___ Am I able to keep my tone of voice from being too harsh or commanding?

___ Was I able to talk and listen to each camper?

___ Was I able to enforce rules and policies of the camp?

___ Did I show enthusiasm and was my attitude positive and encouraging?

___ Did I treat the campers with respect?

___ Am I helping campers to grow intellectually and socially?

___ Did I show honest support of the other staff?

___ Did I help where needed even if it was not my responsibility?

___ Did I maintain a good sense of humor?

___ Did I get enough sleep?

___ Did I eat well?

___ Did I make time for myself?

___ Do I recognize my limits?

___ Is there someone I can confide in?

Your supervisor may have several conferences with you during the summer to help you be more successful at camp. Your self-assessment or your supervisor's evaluation may give you ideas on handling some behavior problems you have been having with your campers or other staff. You may even identify some ideas for in-service training that may help all counselors.

The camp may also have a camper and/or parent evaluation process or form to find out what the campers and their parents felt about the camp experience and how successful the camp was at achieving the camp's goals and outcomes. If these are discussed at a staff meeting before the end of camp, this type of evaluation may give counselors some ideas to use with new campers.

Your experience this summer as a counselor or staff member at camp will help you understand how you work with others and will be an excellent indicator for the future directions you may want to take in your life.

Index